ABBA

ABBA

Nina Rasmussen

AN ORION PAPERBACK

This is a Carlton Book

First published in Great Britain in 1993 by Orion Books Ltd,
Orion House, 5 Upper St Martin's Lane, London WC2H 9EA

A CIP catalogue record for this book is available from the British Library.

ISBN 1 85797 568 5

Edited, designed and typeset by Haldane Mason
Printed in Italy

THE AUTHOR

Nina Rasmussen

Like the erstwhile members of Abba, Nina has spent much of her life living in or near Stockholm, from where she has been able to observe the lives and times of Sweden's most internationally successful musical quartet at close quarters. Her career as a rock and pop journalist has also taken her to London on many occasions since the late 1970s, providing her with a unique viewpoint on the activities of the group members both during and since their incredible career.

CONTENTS

Introduction

Abba made their own piece of pop history as the first pop/rock group from a non-English speaking country to become internationally famous. Between 1974 and 1982, the quartet, which consisted of Benny Andersson (keyboards), Björn Ulvaeus (guitar, vocals), Agnetha Fältskog (vocals) and Anni-Frid Lyngstad (vocals) were among the biggest groups in the world, with a succession of huge international hits that were unequalled during that time. Even more unlikely was the fact that they first came to fame by winning the Eurovision Song Contest, long noted as the least trend-conscious pop event of any year, and therefore a waste of time and an embarrassment.

Abba released nine Number 1 singles in 6½ years, as well as eight

Abba—the sound of the Seventies.

albums which topped the chart in the same period, and it's safe to say that they were the most popular pop group in the world for at least part of that time. Every new Abba release was an event—the sheer catchiness of the songs, with their wonderful choruses which were familiar after being heard just once, the glamour of the girls, the high quality of the videos, all contributed to the group's success. Abba had it made.

When they disbanded in the early Eighties, it seemed unlikely that the group would ever be heard of again except when their hits were played on the radio as golden oldies. Today we know that such a prediction was quite wrong—the quality and excitement of their classic recordings has now been heard and understood by a new generation of record buyers, who regard them as superstars. This is their story.

Left to right: Björn Ulvaeus, Anni-Frid Lyngstad, Agnetha Fältskog and Benny Andersson—Abba.

Chapter One

SECOND TIME AROUND

In 1992 Abba became chart contenders, 10 years after they had effectively split up. With a new generation of teenagers looking for inspiration, Abba were obvious role models.

While Abba weren't really part of the glam rock movement that was spearheaded by Marc Bolan and T Rex, the Sweet, David Bowie (in his Ziggy Stardust era), Slade, Gary Glitter and all the others, Abba were adored by pop fans throughout the Seventies because they were the epitome of glamorous pop stars—they dressed in eye-catching gear and they took hit after perfect pop hit to the top of the charts. They also wrote and sang good songs. As

Left to right: Björn, Anni-Frid, Agnetha, Benny—glamour personified.

Benny once commented, "Our secret—if we have one—is to be completely ruthless about the material we write. If Stig, Björn or I don't like any aspect of one of our songs, we scrap it immediately."

Famous pop stars from the next generation also rated the group highly.

Back in 1984, Blancmange had already had the downright cheek to take an Abba song, 'The Day Before You Came', to a higher position in the chart than the Swedish quartet's original version. However, it wasn't until a couple of unlikely events in 1992 that the Abba revival became more than just wishful thinking.

First came a superior "copy group", Björn Again, a quartet from Australia who had based a very successful career on a live show composed of Abba classics. Taking great care to look and dress like Abba (as best they could—the two girls, Tracy Adams and Annette Jones, had the same hair colour as Agnetha and Anni-Frid, but Gavin Edwards and Peter Smith, Björn and Benny respectively, were slightly less convincing), Björn Again couldn't fail, because they were providing a show that people wanted.

"Our secret—if we have one—is to be completely ruthless about the material we write."
Benny

Björn Again—same gear, new generation, different nationality.

The genuine article wasn't available, as the real Abba hadn't worked together since the start of the Eighties, and even

Bright, eye-catching and highly successful—a vintage shot of Abba in their early days.

when they did, none of the four liked touring that much. Benny liked some aspects: "I do enjoy tours, but not all the travelling and the hotel rooms, and I certainly prefer the creative side of my work. It's much pleasanter for me to create music in the studio than to just reproduce it on stage."

There was a definite demand for a group to play Abba's music and Björn Again got it right, with Tracy and Annette changing their costumes several times during each show so that they looked very like Abba had at various stages of their career. With sharply accurate performances of

> **"It's much pleasanter for me to create music in the studio than to just reproduce it on stage."**
>
> **Benny**

Abba's hits, Björn Again cleaned up, and they're still touring today with hardly a break, filling halls all over Europe. Everybody loves the Australian group—both parents who remember classic hits like 'Dancing Queen', 'Knowing Me, Knowing You', 'Chiquitita', 'Fernando' and all the rest, and teenagers who borrow the old Abba albums they find in the record collections belonging to their mums and dads.

Andy Bell (left) and Vince Clarke of Erasure, who took an EP of covers of Abba's hits to the top of the charts.

Erasure steps in

The next step in the Abba revival occurred when electropop duo Erasure (Vince Clarke and Andy Bell) topped the UK chart with a 4-track EP of Abba songs, which they performed in familiar Erasure style. Already established as one of Britain's most popular acts with a long string of hits to their credit,

including three consecutive UK Number 1 albums—*The Innocents*, *Wild!* and *Chorus*—Erasure had never had a chart-topping single until they made their tribute to the group who had been the soundtrack to their teenage years.

The original plan was to record a complete album of covers of Abba hits, but the pressures of fame allowed Vince and Andy too little time. What eventually emerged was an EP, *Abba-esque*, with just four revivals of familiar Abba classics—'Lay All Your Love On Me', 'S.O.S.', 'Take A Chance On Me' and 'Voulez-Vous'. The EP also topped the charts in many other parts of Europe, where the revival of interest in Abba was equally explosive. (The light-hearted approach of Björn Again was illustrated later that year when they called their first hit single 'Erasure-ish'—it contained their cover versions of hits by Erasure!)

"I don't deal from a money point of view; I see what a company does for us and whether they do it in the right way."
Stig

Agnetha, who took lead vocal on most of Abba's hits, centre stage in the early Seventies.

Legends together

Soon after *Abba-esque* became a smash hit, an even more famous band acknowledged that Abba had been one of their favourite groups during their teenage years. Irish superstars U2 had been playing one of Abba's biggest hits, 'Dancing Queen', as an encore on their world tour—and when that tour reached Stockholm, capital city of Sweden, where Abba had been based during the years when they were rarely absent from the world's charts, Benny and Björn joined the Irish quartet on stage to sing the massive hit they had written well over 10 years before. Their appearance provided an unexpected highlight for an audience who could hardly believe their luck at seeing two legends on stage together.

In fact, something similar had happened earlier in the year in Zurich, Switzerland, when Anni-Frid (who now lives in that country for part of each year), came on stage with Roxette, another Swedish group who have enjoyed major international success, to sing 'Money Money Money' with them. Even so, it remains unlikely that Abba will ever perform together again as they were back in the Seventies,

Anni-Frid, Abba's sexy siren, inflames her audience.

Much of Abba's success was due to their work in the field of promotional videos —as they couldn't visit every country where their hits were released, they supplied videos instead.

despite rumours in the press that offers of vast sums of money have been made for just one more tour. They were two happily married couples at the time of their hits, and the marriages ended in acrimonious divorces—although at the time Agnetha and Björn's separation was described as friendly. According to Agnetha: "We just couldn't live together any longer and we're filing for divorce. When you talk about everything and still fail to get through to each other, then you must take the consequences. We just

Björn (left) and Benny—the songwriting team which chalked up ten UK Number 1s between 1974 and 1985.

"We just couldn't live together any longer and we're filing for divorce. We just grew apart."
Agnetha

A

grew apart." Björn was more impersonal: "This is a friendly separation, if such a thing exists, and there is no reason for Abba to stop performing as a group." Considering this fact, and that the four members of Abba have since forged new partnerships, it simply wouldn't be that easy to try to re-create the past even if they wanted to—which by all accounts they don't.

Behind the stunning stage performances and eye-catching outfits lay plenty of hard work to make sure the fans would hear Abba at their very best.

Abba Gold

By the end of the summer of 1992 there was a growing demand for Abba's music—and that demand was about to be met. In 1990, the group's catalogue of hits had been bought (for an amount that may have topped £10 million/$15 million) by Polygram Records, who became the first international record company to release an Abba album worldwide. Previously, Stig Anderson had made record deals with numerous competing labels around the world: "I don't deal from a money point of view; I see what a company does for us and whether they do it in the right way. I don't believe in worldwide deals—a

B

company can be strong in one region and weak in another. It depends on the people. I go with people I like, and hand pick them territory by territory."

However, in 1990 he finally made the single worldwide deal with Polygram. The result was the multi-million selling *Abba Gold*, a compilation album that topped the charts in at least 15 countries over four continents. This was a "greatest hits" album that included all Abba's nine

Just four people on a stage—but the music they put out packed a punch that made millions fall under their spell.

A

Number 1 singles as well as ten other very familiar favourites.

The record industry could hardly believe it when *Abba Gold* rocketed to the top of the charts in Britain, Germany, Australia, Mexico, Israel, Singapore and other countries and sold an incredible 4 million copies! Highly paid talent scouts had been paying fortunes to sign new groups who seemed to have the potential to become stars, yet here was this Swedish quartet outselling them all—though they hadn't made a new record for 10 years!

Björn—a songwriter of genius who set feet tapping in all four corners of the world.

New lives

Where had the members of Abba been since they were last in the charts at the start of the 1980s? People said they should have played at the Live Aid concert in 1985, where they would have been a huge attraction—but perhaps they weren't asked or perhaps they didn't want to. So what had they been doing?

Benny and Björn, the songwriting team who had produced so many hits, were still working together, although they were living in different countries. Benny was in Sweden with his wife Mona, whom he had married in late 1981, while Björn and his wife, Lena, had bought a country house near Henley in England where they were resident for part of the year. Both Agnetha and Anni-Frid had also remarried—Agnetha had remained single until the end of 1990, when she married surgeon Tomas Sonnenfeld, while Anni-Frid became the wife of Prince Ruzzo Reuss von Plauen, a German architect, in the

Abba under the spotlights again, with all their customary pizzazz.

B

ABBA

In the early Eighties Frida cherished hopes of becoming an international solo star.

summer of 1992, after the couple had lived together for several years. The four one-time members of Abba had not worked together since 1986, when they had reunited on film to record a Swedish song written by their manager, Stig Anderson. This appearance was included in a TV tribute to Anderson, who had been responsible for planning much of their success and who had actually coined the name under which they had found worldwide stardom.

A new track

Following the success of *Abba Gold*, there had been considerable activity in all matters relating to Abba. Apart from the album itself, a companion video had also topped the chart, as had an authorized book about the group, all sharing the same title.

Agnetha discovered that after the success of Abba solo stardom was not an easy option.

By the middle of 1993 a follow-up album had been released—*More Abba Gold*, which, while it inevitably wasn't quite as packed with huge hits as the first album, entered

the Top 20 of the UK album chart as soon as it was available, confirming that the Abba revival was an ongoing event.

The one very special aspect of this second album was that it included a track which had never previously been released, 'I Am The City'. This was not a newly recorded item but one that the group had made shortly before they took their decision that there would be no further new Abba albums. None the less, Abba fans were delighted that there was at least one new recording available with the Abba magic that had been absent from the singles chart for so long. And who knows, the Abba story may still not have reached its end!

"This is a friendly separation, if such a thing exists, and there is no reason for Abba to stop performing as a group."

Björn

Benny enjoys the fame restored by the success of *Abba Gold*.

Chapter Two

A

THE FLEDGLING FOUR

As every Abba fan knows, the name Abba is made up of the initial letters of the first name of each member of the group—Agnetha Fältskog, Björn Ulvaeus, Benny Andersson and Anni-Frid Lyngstad.

Agnetha Fältskog, the youngest member of Abba, was born in Jönköping, a town in the south of Sweden, in 1950. Encouraged by her father, she first performed on stage before she was 7 years old. By the time she was 15 she was singing with a local dance band, and 2 years on she was discovered by a talent scout.

In early 1968, she had a recording contract and was filled with excitement as the song which had impressed the talent scout became her very first single and topped the charts in Sweden. This was not a bad start, and the young blonde beauty built on it by releasing a succession of hit singles and albums until she was one of the biggest stars in Sweden, making frequent appearances on television.

The teenage Agnetha, whose first single topped the Swedish chart when she was only 18.

In 1969, Agnetha's life took a new turn when she encountered a fellow Swedish pop star, the singer and guitarist Björn Ulvaeus. Their meeting was the start of something which would change the course of pop history.

Björn's beginnings

Twenty-four-year-old Björn came from Västervik, on the east coast of Sweden—although he was born in Gothenburg, on the west coast. He was a member of a folk group at school who were big fans of the Kingston Trio, a successful American folk band who had hits with songs like 'Tom Dooley'.

Named the West Bay Singers, in 1963 the group went on a touring holiday around Europe, and on their return to Sweden entered a talent contest, attracting the interest of a local music publisher, Stig Anderson. He invited them to audition and quickly signed the group, who by now were called the Hootenanny Singers. They soon became regular entrants to the local chart.

It seemed that the group's success might be interrupted by a period of conscription in the Swedish

Björn in pre-Abba days. While at university, Björn would supplement his grant by composing songs on his guitar.

army, but they were allowed to continue with their musical career as long as they also completed their army training at the same time. After that the group members went to university, and, when he was not studying, Björn spent his spare time working as a songwriter for Polar Music, the company launched by Stig Anderson.

In 1967, the Hootenanny Singers played a concert in the same Swedish town as another well-known group, the Hep Stars. It was here that Björn met the Hep Stars' young keyboards player, Benny Andersson. They got on so well together that they decided to write a song, 'Isn't It Easy To Say', which was later recorded by the Hep Stars. Another piece of the Abba jigsaw was falling into place.

Benny Andersson was the first member of Abba to find stardom—he was the keyboard player with the successful Swedish group the Hep Stars.

"When I look back at the Hep Stars, I realize we used to play a sort of country and western with a German beat, if you can imagine that. At the time, we thought we were an up-to-the-minute rock group."

Benny

A natural talent

Benny Andersson was born near Stockholm in 1946. Both his father and grandfather were interested in music, and Benny was given an accordion when he was only 6 years old.

One of his great talents, even as a child, was the ability to get a tune out of just about any instrument he picked up.

In the Sixties Benny joined the Hep Stars, a Swedish rock group, who played "a sort of country and western with a German beat, if you can imagine that," as Benny put it later. "At the time, we thought we were an up-to-the-minute rock group, and luckily, that's what everybody else seemed to think we were."

In the autumn of 1964 the group took off in a big way after a wild appearance on television. For the next 3 years they were Sweden's biggest rock stars, scoring many hits—several of which were written by Benny. Unfortunately, they foolishly spent all the money and never thought about income tax. The inevitable occurred, and after receiving a huge tax bill of about £100,000 ($150,000), they had to work extremely hard to pay off their debt and avoid a heavy fine on top of the small fortune they already owed.

By the middle of 1969 Benny had left the Hep Stars—but not before he had worked again with Björn, whom he had invited to guest with the group when their full-time guitarist was late returning from a vacation. Another step was taken towards a world-beating partnership.

The sleeve of an early solo album by Anni-Frid, a couple of years before Abba.

The girl from Narvik

It's generally believed that Abba is a totally Swedish group, but in fact that isn't quite correct. Anni-Frid Lyngstad (known as Frida) was the one member of Abba who wasn't Swedish. She was born in Narvik, a town just inside the Arctic Circle in Norway, in 1945. Her mother died before Frida was 2 years old, and her father, a German soldier named Alfred Haase, had returned to Germany at the end of the Second World War unaware that his love affair with a young Norwegian girl was to make him a father.

The people of Narvik strongly disapproved of a Norwegian girl producing a child by an enemy soldier; Frida's mother was left friendless, lost her grasp on life and died in deep despair. Frida's grandmother, left to look after the toddler, decided to move far away from Narvik to give her granddaughter a new start in life. In 1947 they crossed the border into Sweden. After travelling around the country for a few years, the pair finally settled in Eskilstuna, a town not far from Stockholm.

The creation of a future Number 1? Benny (at the piano) and Björn at a song-writing session.

Even before Frida was a teenager, it was obvious that she had potential as a singer. While she was still only 13 years old, she was the featured vocalist with a dance band, and went on to sing with a big band, forming a relationship with one of the other members. The couple eventually left to form a small group, the Anni-Frid Four, who were fairly popular locally.

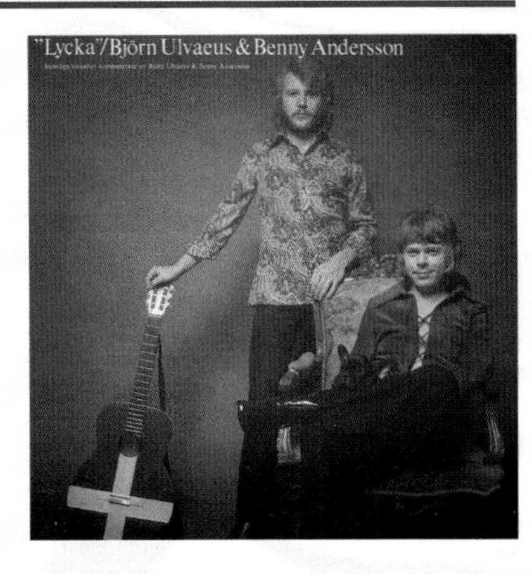

Benny and Björn's *Lycka* album, released in 1970.

Frida had two children, which prevented her being able to sing in front of an audience as often as she would have liked. None the less, she won a talent contest in 1967, and appeared on a popular TV show. Bitten by the showbiz bug, Frida left her husband and children and moved to Stockholm, the centre of the Swedish music industry. After signing with a record label, she became a well-known recording artist.

Her life changed when she was performing at a night club in Malmö, in the extreme south of Sweden. The Hep Stars were appearing at another club in town, and she met Benny Andersson. Their professional lives brought Benny and Frida together again and again—and romance blossomed when they appeared together on a radio quiz show in 1970. Together with Björn and Agnetha, they were to write a substantial new chapter in the history of popular music.

Two plus two

At the start of the Seventies, Benny and Björn began to work as a duo more seriously. They had left the groups with which they had found fame and together they wrote and recorded 'She's My Kind Of Girl', which was a huge hit in Japan, where it sold half a million copies. They also recorded an album together (in Swedish), entitled *Lycka*. By the time the album was released in 1970 Benny and Frida had become engaged, and their example was quickly followed by Björn and Agnetha.

During this period, the two men continued to work together while each tried to assist the solo career of his fiancée. The idea of working as a quartet didn't occur until the end of 1970, when Benny and Björn were appearing together in Gothenberg. Neither Agnetha nor Anni-Frid was working that evening, so it was decided that all four should perform as a group under the name of Festfolk, which can either mean engaged couples or party-goers—perhaps both meanings were appropriate. Unfortunately, the

Benny and Frida, engaged in 1970, not married till 1978!

Agnetha and Björn, who also got engaged in 1970, were married the following year.

quickly prepared act they had put together for the evening was quite wrong for the audience, and the four decided that the experiment had been a failure.

Benny and Björn returned to songwriting, one of their major successes coming

ABBA

Left: The four as Abba, with a rare shot of Anni-Frid's briefly seen perm.

Right: The better-looking half of Abba: Anni-Frid (left) and Agnetha.

when French pop and film star Françoise Hardy recorded a song they had written, called 'Language Of Love'.

Meanwhile, Agnetha worked in the theatre, playing the part of Mary Magdalene in a Swedish version of the Tim Rice/ Andrew Lloyd Webber musical *Jesus Christ Superstar*. She also released her version of one of the major songs from the show, 'I Don't Know How To Love Him', which became a big hit in Sweden.

During this period Anni-Frid carried on with her solo career, releasing a new album in Swedish, titled *Min Egen Stad*.

New partnerships

After much searching around the Swedish countryside for a sufficiently romantic setting for their wedding ceremony, Björn and Agnetha found an ancient Gothic church in southern Sweden. On the day of the marriage in July, 1971, the small building was packed and large crowds waited outside for this celebrity love match. The only cloud to darken an almost perfect day was the

Happy days for the soon-to-be Swedish superstars.

suicide of a longtime professional partner of Stig Anderson who was suffering from an incurable disease. Even this had its positive side—Stig now needed a new partner, and the obvious choice was Björn. However, Björn had such belief in his partnership with Benny that he told Stig he would only agree to this proposal if Benny also became a partner. Stig couldn't afford to pay them both, and after some negotiation Björn and Benny agreed to Stig's suggestion that they should share a single salary.

Left to right: Benny, Agnetha, Björn and Anni-Frid—the image that launched scores of hits.

In late 1971, almost a year after the Festfolk fiasco, the two couples decided to have another try at working as a quartet. This time it was much more successful, but another problem prevented further experimentation—the record company to which Agnetha was signed exclusively would not allow a single she made with Björn to be released on Polar, the record company to which Björn was under contract, and this delayed the record for some time. When it was finally released, it was far from new. Even so, the news wasn't all bad. Because 'She's My Kind Of Girl' had been such a big hit for Björn and Benny in Japan, they were invited to enter a song

for the Japanese Song Festival. Agnetha and Frida went with them, and all four of them performed the song 'Santa Rosa', which was given a positive reception by the judges at the festival.

The first record

When they returned to Stockholm Björn and Benny wrote and recorded a new song, 'People Need Love', on which the girls assisted with the vocals. Because the two female voices were featured so prominently, Björn and Benny insisted that Agnetha and Frida should be credited on the label of the record. If Stig wondered whether Björn And Benny might be too Swedish for an international audience, he was sure that calling the group Björn, Benny, Agnetha And Frida would kill any chance the single might have of becoming a success, particularly in America, where Playboy Records, an offshoot of the men's magazine, was interested in releasing it.

Eventually a compromise was reached—the record was credited to Björn And Benny with Svenska Flicka, and came close to reaching the US pop chart when Playboy released it. Problems with distribution eventually prevented the single from reaching the Hot 100, but it was still the biggest-ever US single by a Swedish act up to that time.

Both 'People Need Love' and a follow-up single, 'He Is Your Brother', were massive hits in Sweden, and it was becoming obvious that this newly formed group, who were still without a name, were among the biggest stars in the country.

Grand ambitions

Stig Anderson still had ambitions—he reckoned that the songs that Benny and Björn were writing were good enough to become hits outside Scandinavia, and maybe in America, something which had never been achieved by a record from Sweden.

His first real chance to find out whether he was right came when the Swedish Broadcasting Corporation invited Björn and Benny to submit a song for the competition to decide the Swedish entry for the 1973 Eurovision Song Contest. The contest

B

would be viewed by a huge TV audience all over Europe, allowing Björn, Benny, Agnetha and Frida to be seen by audiences in Britain, France, Germany and Holland, which would be a big step on the road to having hits in those countries.

And this is where the story of Abba really begins.

The name "Abba" came from the initial letters of Agnetha, Björn, Benny and Anni-Frid.

Chapter Three

ABBA COME OF AGE

Both Anni-Frid and particularly Agnetha were well-known stars in Sweden, while Björn and Benny were famous from their days in successful groups and had already proved that they could write hits. Aided by Stig, who at the time wrote better English lyrics, they composed 'Ring Ring', which they entered in the contest to decide the Swedish entry for the Eurovision Song Contest.

The competition took place in February, in the same month and almost on the same day that Agnetha was expecting her first child to arrive. Anni-Frid learned all the female vocal parts of the song so that Agnetha's voice would not be missed if she was hospitalized on the day. Even if Agnetha hadn't given birth before the performance, her pregnancy would be a

Abba at the 1973 Swedish Eurovision heat, with Agnetha very pregnant.

Björn and Benny and their other halves were an obvious choice to write and perform the 1973 Swedish entry for the Eurovision Song Contest.

The sleeve for the first Abba single, 'Ring Ring', the song which was undeservedly rejected as the Swedish entry for the Eurovision Song Contest.

talking point which might work in the group's favour. As it happened, Linda Elin Ulvaeus did not appear until nearly 2 weeks after the group's unexpected and undeserved failure to win the Eurovision heat.

Surprise rejection

There was absolutely no doubt that the audience watching the contest felt that 'Ring Ring' should have won—its light-hearted message about talking on the telephone, performed in a style comparable with contemporary British or American stars, was streets ahead of its rivals, and when it was placed only third by a panel of judges there was a public outcry. The judges were clearly out of touch with trends in popular music, and it was decided that in future years the winner of the competition would be the song which the public most favoured, not one chosen by "experts" who didn't have a feel for modern pop music.

No one seems to remember the song that was chosen to represent Sweden that year, but whatever it

Stig Anderson (left) explains his plan for domination of the world's charts to Abba.

was it certainly didn't win the actual Eurovision contest and Sweden's sad record of never having produced a Eurovision winner was maintained for yet another year. Stig Anderson had possibly been over-confident, but because 'Ring Ring' had been such a hot favourite he had made advance plans to capitalize on what he felt was virtually a certain hit by also getting Abba to record the song with lyrics in three other European languages—English, German and Spanish. Even when it was rejected by the Swedish judges, he was able to get the song released as a single in several other countries, crucially including Britain, where it eventually came out later in 1973. However, it still failed to launch Abba's career in Britain—that would take another year.

Abba is born

By this time the somewhat clumsy group name of Björn, Benny, Agnetha And Frida had been replaced by the much simpler and more memorable Abba, apparently coined by Stig Anderson during interviews with journalists. Finding that calling the quartet by their four names lacked punch, he created the word Abba out of the initial letters of their first names. Of course, he could have called them Baba, or even Fabb, if he had used Frida's shortened name rather than the full Anni-Frid!

His only problem after settling on Abba was that a famous Swedish company noted for its superior range of canned fish was also called Abba, and he was worried that the sardine sultans might not let him share the name. However, after they were reassured that the group would not cheapen their name the company gave the go-ahead—which probably resulted in far more international exposure for Abba's fishy fare than they could ever have expected.

The version of 'Ring Ring' which was released in Britain (where it was a total flop) was not the one that had been recorded before the Swedish Eurovision heat fiasco. Stig had contacted famous American hit-maker

The group had plenty to look happy about—they'd found a catchy name and their career was building fast.

Neil Sedaka and asked him to improve the song's lyrics, which Sedaka duly did with his songwriting partner of the time, Phil Cody. However, not even Sedaka could make the song into a UK hit, although the single reached Number 1 in Holland and Belgium as well as the Scandinavian countries, and was also later a chart-topper in Australia and South Africa. The word about Abba was beginning to spread.

A second attempt

Encouraged by the single's runaway success, Stig Anderson began to make plans for Abba to represent Sweden in the 1974 Eurovision Contest, confident that they would have a far better chance of success now that the method of choosing the Swedish entry reflected popularity rather than prejudice. Benny and Björn started thinking about an appropriate song at the end of 1973, and Stig in particular saw the need for it to have a title that could be universally recognized in every part of the world.

After some discussion about a song they had written called 'Hasta Manana', which most people understand means "see you soon" or "see you tomorrow", Stig eventually chose 'Waterloo'. The famous battle at which Napoleon was defeated in

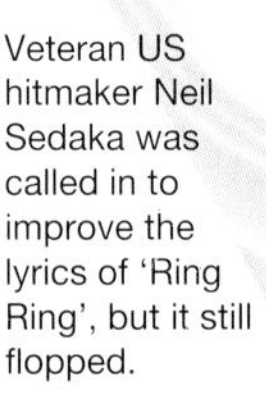

Veteran US hitmaker Neil Sedaka was called in to improve the lyrics of 'Ring Ring', but it still flopped.

1815 was well known throughout the Western world, and Björn and Benny constructed a cheerful and lively tune to match lyrics which compared the French emperor's surrender to a woman's romantic surrender to a lover. It was an obvious improvement on 'Ring Ring' and when the quartet performed it in the Swedish Eurovision heat it won an overwhelming popular victory, gaining more votes than all the other entries put together.

In order to give themselves the best possible chance when it came to the Eurovision final, which was due to be held in Brighton, on the south coast of England, the group looked for eye-catching stage clothes so that they could make as big an impression as possible on the international juries who would decide the winner of the song contest. They also devised an amusing additional feature which still remains memorable even two decades later—Sven-Olof Waldoff, conductor of the orchestra which was to back the group, was persuaded to wear a distinctive Napoleon-style hat. With a good song, bright clothes and Sven-Olof Waldoff's hat (as well as Bjorn's guitar, which was shaped like a star), they were ready to take on the whole of Europe—and maybe even the world.

Abba (in the foreground) ignore Napoleon —who lost the battle of 'Waterloo' while Abba beat the rest of Europe.

A

Waterloo!

Stig Anderson made sure that his contacts all over Europe knew about 'Waterloo' and the song was released in a number of countries even before the Eurovision contest took place. Stig is a very methodical operator with considerable experience in the music industry. He has four rules by which he lives: "Always work very hard, do your best, don't forget anything and don't take life too seriously."

When the Abba party arrived in England their song was strongly fancied to win the contest. The

The winning team—Abba with Stig Anderson (back row, centre) and Sven-Olof Waldoff (with hat) at Brighton in 1974.

Abba in London's Hyde Park as Eurovision winners in April, 1974.

British entry was to be sung by Olivia Newton-John, however, and although it was a fairly average song entitled 'Long Live Love', Olivia's fame was such that she had become the favourite the day before the contest. None the less, justice was done and Abba won the contest beyond all doubt, thus launching their international career in spectacular style.

'Waterloo' was so popular that it topped the singles chart in the UK and over a dozen other countries, although perhaps its greatest achievement was in reaching the Top 10 in America on the back of its success in Britain. Very few European acts had made a major impact in the States before Abba—there had been occasional one-off hits, like 'Venus' by the Dutch group Shocking Blue, which had been a US Number 1 back in 1969 (and which reached Number 1 again when Bananarama revived the song in 1986), but such occurrences were very rare, and certainly no Swedish act had ever done as well before Abba.

"Always work very hard, do your best, don't forget anything and don't take life too seriously."

Stig

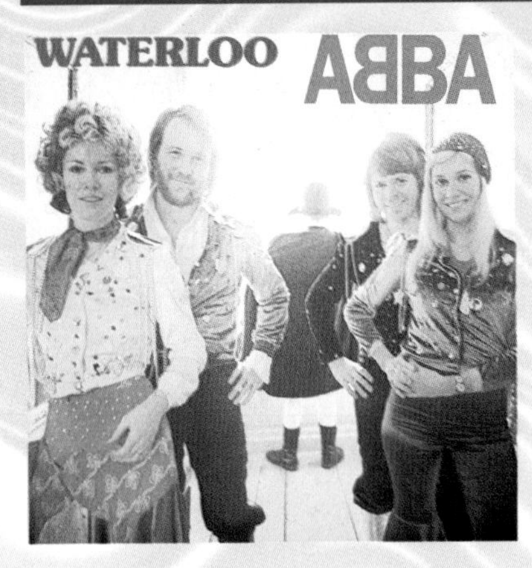

The *Waterloo* album, Abba's first to be released in the UK.

Back down to earth

Perhaps because of the generally accepted view of the Eurovision Song Contest among record buyers in Britain, who regarded it as little more than a joke, Abba initially found it difficult to build on the great success enjoyed by 'Waterloo'. After all, apart from the British and Irish entries, none of the previous winners of the contest had ever managed to follow up a Eurovision winner with another hit of any note, and the list of artists who had only been famous for at best a few weeks was long. The general feeling was that, while any song which won the Eurovision contest might be a hit in Europe, the artist involved was highly unlikely to reach such heights again. Until Abba changed the history of pop music this view was entirely accurate.

It looked at first as though this long-established precedent would also apply to Abba. Their *Waterloo* album made a very brief chart appearance for only 2 weeks, and their follow-up single only just managed to limp into the UK Top 40 before giving up the ghost.

The track chosen as this all-important follow-up was 'Ring Ring', the song that had been rejected by the Swedish judges a year earlier and ignored when it was released in Britain a few months before 'Waterloo'. It may not have

B

been an inspired choice—but worse was to follow.

In the run-up to Christmas, 1974, another Abba single was released, which fared even less well. 'So Long' was probably a better bet than 'Ring Ring', but while it was a hit in some European countries it totally failed in the UK and seems not to have been released in America as a single at all.

Surprisingly, the group were more successful in following up the Top 10 status of 'Waterloo' in the US, where a track from the *Waterloo* album, 'Honey

Left: Finally international stars, Abba were happy—but even bigger success wasn't far away.

Overleaf: The four back in Sweden, relaxed and enjoying the fruits of their labours.

PRINCETON

Honey', became a Top 30 hit. 'Honey Honey' was also a hit in Britain, although not for Abba. Written by Benny and Björn, it was recorded by an English duo known as Sweet Dreams, whose version became their only hit when it reached the Top 10.

"It's very difficult for us to get away from the Eurovision tag, especially in England, where people seem to expect us to produce records in the 'Waterloo' vein."

Björn

A change of style with the nostalgic 'I Do, I Do, I Do, I Do, I Do' hardly improved Abba's standing.

A change of style

Abba spent the end of 1974 and the beginning of 1975 licking their wounds and wondering how to rebuild their reputation, which had been severely tarnished by their two failures. They decided on a change of style for the next single, with a song that was far from the pop/rock sound of 'Waterloo' and in fact seemed more like something from the era before rock 'n' roll. 'I Do, I Do, I Do, I Do, I Do' was not the kind of track that would appeal to the teenagers and young adults who made up most of Abba's following at the time, and it was even

less of a hit than 'Ring Ring'. At this point Abba were starting to be written off as typical Eurovision fodder; as Björn said, "It's very difficult for us to get away from the Eurovision tag, especially in England, where people seem to expect us to produce records in the 'Waterloo' vein." It was hard to argue with such judgements—especially when their new album, simply titled *Abba*, was released in the early summer of 1975.

The second album appeared to be another failure, and for a long time was conspicuous by its absence from the UK charts—although this state of affairs would change by the end of the year. None the less, it was considerably superior to *Waterloo*, displaying a confidence and variety that far surpassed its comparatively mundane predecessor.

Unfortunately, because the only tracks that were familiar to record buyers when the album was released were the group's previous two singles, the disappointing 'I Do, I Do, I Do, I Do, I Do', and 'So Long', it was generally ignored, although reviewers noted that at least two of the new songs, 'S.O.S.' and 'Mamma Mia', were an improvement.

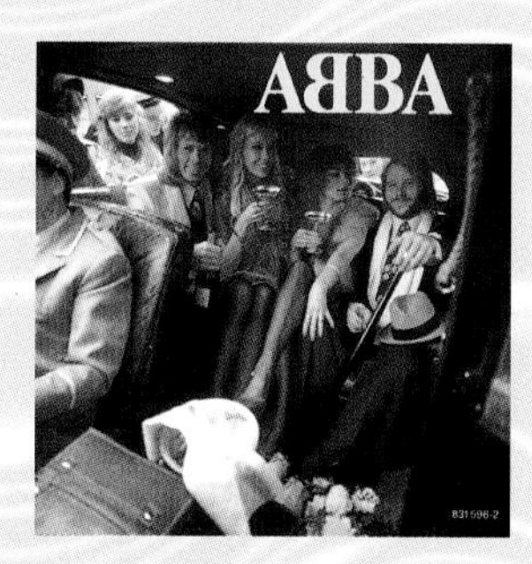

The second album, simply titled *Abba*, set records in Sweden and included the next two smash singles.

In Sweden, where Abba remained heroes, it was a quite different story. Never before had any album attracted advance orders of 150,000 copies, and by the end of 1975, when half a million Swedes had bought it, it was estimated that 1 person in every 20 in the entire country had a copy. This was a remarkable statistic, and if a similar percentage of the population of Britain had purchased the album, its sales would have been around 3 million copies!

Behind the Iron Curtain

Around this time it became clear that Abba's international appeal was wider than anyone had suspected. A visit to Sweden by a politician from Poland was widely reported in Polish newspapers, and this included a mention of Abba, with the address of their fan club in Sweden. Soon thousands of letters poured into Sweden from pop fans in Poland, which was the start of one of Abba's more interesting achievements—for at that time Poland was still behind the Iron Curtain, where pop music was frowned upon. Before long more Eastern European countries were to fall under the quartet's spell. Abba's music had given the people of Poland, the then East Germany and even Russia a taste of Western pop music which was far more interesting than the local fare, where electric guitars and light-hearted songs with catchy choruses were virtually unknown.

Livening up the airwaves of Eastern Europe when the Berlin Wall was still standing.

'S.O.S.' hits the big time

Abba's next single was released during the autumn of 1975, almost 18 months after they had hit the jack-pot with 'Waterloo'. The failures of 'Ring Ring', 'So Long' and 'I Do, I Do, I Do, I Do, I Do' were forgotten when 'S.O.S.' crashed into the UK Top 10 only days after it was released. What was more, it also consolidated the group's status in America, where it became their second Top 20 hit, and led to them making a trip across the Atlantic to appear on television.

'S.O.S.' was the first single for which Abba made a promotional video. As they amassed more and more hits during the rest of the Seventies, their eye-catching promo videos would become a major factor in their continuing success. As the demand increased for the four to visit countries where their records were in the chart it became impossible to keep pace. Abba were able to satisfy many requests for personal appearances by supplying a copy of a video clip, a comparatively new concept at that time.

As the group celebrated Christmas in 1975, they could reflect that their fall from grace had been reversed by 'S.O.S.'. They could hardly have realized how successful they would become in the next year.

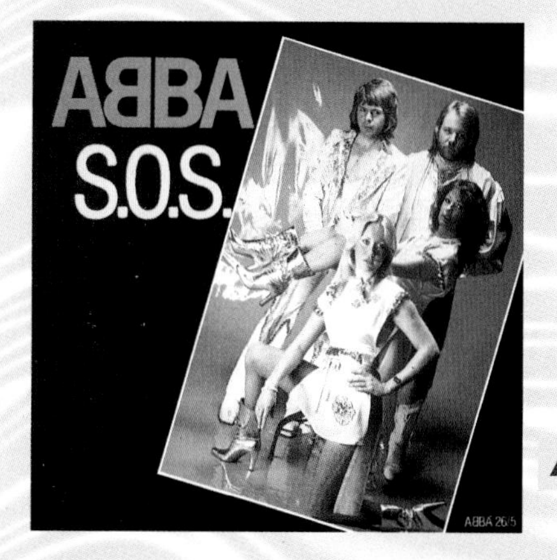

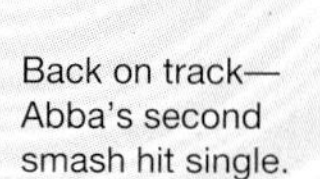
Back on track—
Abba's second
smash hit single.

Chapter Four

A

THE GOLDEN YEARS

Having successfully overcome the problem of following up their Eurovision-winning hit, Abba were on top of the world at the end of 1975.

The *Abba* album released 6 months before had finally started selling in the wake of the Top 10 success of 'S.O.S.', and another single was poised to become even more successful. The opening track of the album, 'Mamma Mia', swiftly entered the UK chart, but was kept from the Number 1 slot by Queen's 'Bohemian Rhapsody', which occupied the top position for an incredible 9 weeks. By the time Freddie and Co's single ran out of steam, 'Mamma Mia' had been in the charts for 7 weeks, the last 2 of them in the Top 3, yet the Abba track still had enough life left in it to climb to pole position for 2 weeks, convincing even the most cynical critic that Abba should be seen as more than probably dubious Eurovision winners.

As the single became their second Number 1 in under 2 years, the *Abba* album finally reached the UK charts as well, where it remained for nearly 3

Abba pictured in the streets of Stockholm.

months. Although it had taken some time, no one could now dispute that Abba were big news.

'Mamma Mia' was also the single which first made Abba superstars in Australia, where for several years the group were almost regarded as deities; at one point there were five singles by Abba simultaneously in the Australian Top 10, and a locally compiled album, *Best of Abba*, sold almost a million copies—in a country with a population of only 14 million!

Finally on stage in Australia, where Abba had been superstars since 'Mamma Mia'.

The third Number 1

In mid-1976 'Mamma Mia' also became Abba's fifth US Top 40 hit in under 2 years, an amazing achievement for a group from a non-English speaking country—although by this time Abba had abandoned recording in any language other than English. When Benny was asked about this later he said, "Why should we bother to record in Swedish? Everyone buys our English versions in Sweden anyway."

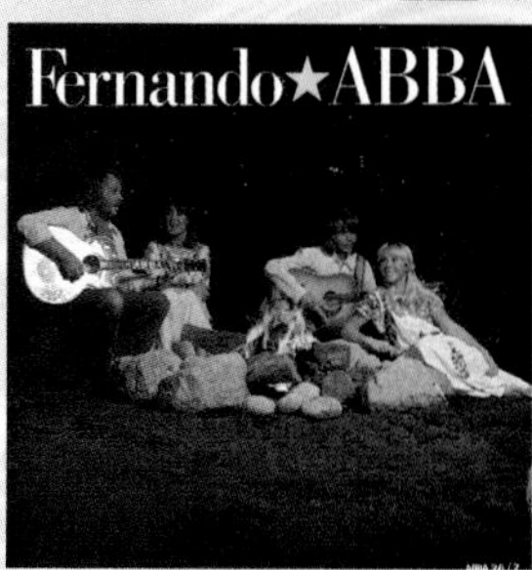

Can you hear the drums, Fernando? Abba's third Number 1.

The bizarre cover of Abba's *Greatest Hits* album.

The group further consolidated their position with another international Number 1 single, 'Fernando'—although once again there was a delay of several weeks before it reached its rightful place at the top of the UK chart. Ironically, the single which held Abba up this time was by a group who were widely believed to have based their entire approach on the blueprint so successfully established by Abba. Not only were Brotherhood Of Man another two-male, two-female group, they were launched into the big time by winning the Eurovision Song Contest with 'Save Your Kisses For Me'. In all honesty, this

song could hardly be termed as innovative as 'Waterloo', yet its somewhat sentimental approach obviously had a particular appeal to British record buyers, who kept it at Number 1 for 6 weeks before Abba's single (which was generally regarded as superior) overtook it.

Down under

Around the time that 'Fernando' was released Abba finally visited Australia, where their arrival caused a sensation. During that trip, which was made purely for promotional purposes rather than to

Björn Again's version of the *Greatest Hits* cover shot.

A

play concerts, the group made a TV special which was reportedly watched by more Australians than had tuned in to the 1969 Apollo 11 space mission when Neil Armstrong took the giant leap for mankind on to the moon. The size of the audiences they attracted proved how popular Abba

> **"Winning Eurovision was like Sweden winning the World Cup"**
>
> **Björn**

had become in Australia, and was almost certainly the reason for today's Abba clones, Björn Again, forming in the first place.

Not just the fabulous four—a rhythm section consolidates the Abba sound.

The syndrome of so-called copy groups such as the Australian Doors and Björn Again appears to have begun in Australia, a country where few British or American bands could be bothered to play concerts on a regular basis, as a result of which the locals formed often impressively convincing bands to play the music of their absent heroes. Björn Again quickly struck gold.

A royal request

The next item on the agenda was a new Abba album, whose title some critics initially found suspect. *Greatest Hits*? Surely Abba hadn't been around long enough? But British record buyers weren't concerned by such details—this was a new Abba album, which

B

certainly did include all their hits up to that point (six, including 'Fernando', the third of their UK Number 1 singles) plus the pick of their two previous albums and a number of early Swedish hits which had never previously been heard in the UK, such as 'People Need Love' and its follow-up from 1972, 'He Is Your Brother'.

Greatest Hits spent longer in the UK album chart than any of Abba's other releases—a staggering 130 weeks (2½ years!), 11 of them at Number 1—and sold over 3 million copies. It seemed that 1976 was shaping up to become the year when Stig Anderson's dreams of Abba dominating the world of pop music were becoming reality.

A highlight of a different sort occurred in June 1976, when Abba were the only musicians from the pop world to be invited to perform at a gala in celebration of the wedding of King Carl Gustaf of Sweden to Silvia Sommerlath. This was some recognition of what great ambassadors for Sweden Abba had become—as Björn had once remarked, "Winning Eurovision was like Sweden winning the World Cup"—but they deserved more of an accolade as the first pop superstars from Sweden.

The four worked hard to create a coordinated image.

When interviewed by *Variety* magazine in 1976, Stig felt that "the only reaction we've had from Sweden has been a letter from the ambassador for Australia. In England, we would have been honoured by the Queen long ago."

The group were able to unveil a new song for the occasion which was entirely appropriate. Although they later protested that 'Dancing Queen' had not been specifically tailored for the royal wedding, and had actually been conceived 6 months before, Abba performed the song before the royal couple to great appreciation. Inevitably, it became their next single a few weeks later.

By this time it was certain that any new release by Abba would become a huge hit. 'Dancing Queen' soared up the British chart and within 2 weeks was at Number 1, where it remained immovable for 6 weeks. During its first month on release it sold half a million copies, and almost certainly exceeded sales of 1 million eventually, a rare occurrence for any single in the UK. It also topped the charts of most other

By 1976, every new Abba single was a guaranteed international smash hit.

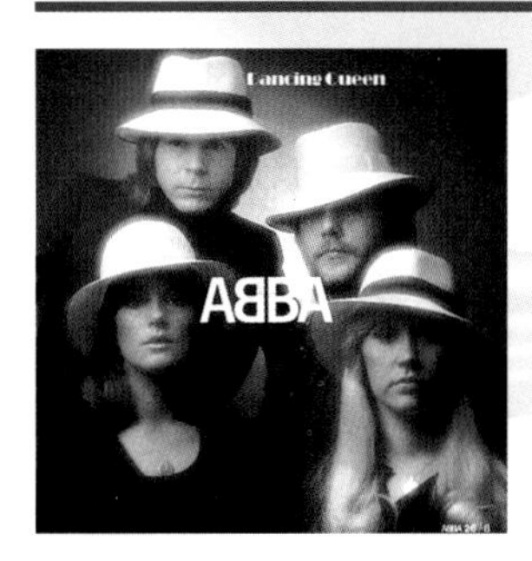

'Dancing Queen', Abba's biggest US hit.

countries in Europe, as well as (inevitably) Australia. More importantly, it became Abba's first (and, to date, only) US Number 1 and first million-selling single in the United States, where it was their seventh Top 40 hit in less than 3 years. This was Abba's third consecutive UK Number 1 and their fourth in all, placing them in the Top 20 of the most prolific and successful hit-makers of all time in the UK—and they had hardly started!

Preparing for the world tour

The next major Abba news concerned their long-awaited world tour, which it was announced would take place at the start of 1977. As the group wanted to re-create the sound of their records as accurately as possible, they began assembling a band which finally included 20 musicians and singers including themselves, while

Abba rehearsing for their first world tour, with Agnetha on vocals.

at the same time Björn and Benny were applying the finishing touches to a new album.

Interleaved with this activity was a promotional trip to the USA. As Abba's singles were often released several months later in the States than in the rest of the world, because they were on different labels, the hit they were promoting at that time was 'Fernando', which was then in the US Top 20—the 'Dancing Queen' triumph was still 6 months or more away.

The group's visit created considerable interest in the US, and among their many activities during the trip was an appearance on a TV show hosted by singer Dinah Shore, who invited

Abba disembark from the personalized plane which they used while on tour.

Benny and Anni-Frid to end their engagement (which by then had lasted several years) by getting married on camera in front of America's huge TV audience. However, the offer was declined, the two agreeing that "if we thought it would improve our relationship, we would get married tomorrow, but as it is, nearly 7 years after we got engaged, we're content to wait. Perhaps we'll get married when we have the time—we're very busy people, you know."

"If we thought it would improve our relationship, we would get married tomorrow, but as it is, nearly 7 years after we got engaged, we're content to wait."

Benny

When the new album, *Arrival*, finally reached the British shops it had already created a record, as it had attracted the biggest advance orders ever for an album in the UK—300,000 copies, which was 30 per cent more than the previous biggest advance sale (for *Horizon*, the 1975 album by the Carpenters). *Arrival* topped the UK album chart soon after its release, eventually spending 10 weeks at Number 1 during a period of nearly 2 years in the chart. It also became the first Abba album to reach the Top 20 in the US, and was their first to be certified gold for sales of 500,000 copies (although the earlier *Greatest Hits* album later outsold it and went platinum with over 1 million sales). *Arrival* not only included 'Dancing Queen', the group's most recent hit single, but also premiered the tracks which

The record-breaking *Arrival* album—300,000 advance sales!

Abba were now a foursome with a Midas touch.

would become their next two singles.

The first of these was 'Money, Money, Money', which featured Anni-Frid as lead vocalist and was supported by a very inventive video. Perhaps because so many British record buyers already owned the track on the *Arrival* album, it was a comparative flop by Abba's high standards, failing to reach Number 1, although it did make the Top 3. But there could be no question of the group's popularity starting to fade—when tickets went on sale for Abba's forthcoming British début concerts at the end of the year more than 3 million applications were received for the 10,000 seats available! Clearly, the tour was going to be a triumph, and the four spent the winter months ensuring that they had considered every possibility.

On the road

The first shows of the tour were in continental Europe, and were predictably received ecstatically. Just before the vitally important British dates, another new single was released—'Knowing Me, Knowing You', which was already familiar to the group's fans, as it was also included on *Arrival*. However, that didn't stop it becoming yet another Number 1 and staying at the top for 5 weeks in the wake of the totally triumphant tour.

The highlight of Abba's live show for many was the inclusion of three new songs from what Benny and Björn called a "mini-musical", *The Girl With the Golden Hair*. The most immediately

"I can't understand how some groups tour for 8, 9, even 10 months—it would kill me."
Björn

B

Abba's fifth Number 1 single, in the chart for 3 months.

popular song of the three was 'Thank You For The Music', which later proved to be perhaps the most familiar song in Abba's repertoire, although it was never a huge hit single. For the part of their live show which included these new songs Agnetha and Anni-Frid were identically dressed and both wore blonde wigs, making it virtually impossible to tell them apart.

The tour continued in Australia, where Abba were guaranteed a wildly enthusiastic reception. Because they were so hugely popular there Stig Anderson decided to film the Australian leg of the tour for possible use in a feature film about the group, and footage was also shot of a rather unconvincing story line, which involved an Australian DJ (played by comedian Robert Hughes) being given an assignment to interview Abba.

While hugely popular and successful in terms of the group's career, financially the tour was less rewarding. In an interview with *Record Mirror* in 1977 Björn revealed that "we didn't make any money at

One of the innumerable Abba press conferences—if it's Tuesday, it must be Peru!

A

all from the tour, in fact we lost, despite every concert being sold out. We didn't enjoy it much anyway, it was boring—all that time confined to hotel rooms. It's healthy to stand on stage and perform, but I can't understand how some groups tour for 8, 9, even 10 months—it would kill me." That feeling was shared by other three members of Abba.

'The Name Of The Game'

By the time the tour had finished another single was due. A new album was also expected, which would include the three tracks from the mini-musical, one of

A matching pair—Agnetha and Anni-Frid with blonde wigs.

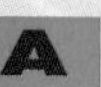

which, 'I Wonder (Departure)', was chosen as the B side of the new single. The A side, 'The Name Of The Game', was also to be on the new album, and as a taster of what Abba fans might expect on the group's fifth album since their rise to fame it was perfect—another great song with a memorable chorus to which anyone could sing along after a single hearing. No one was surprised when it burst into the UK chart during its first week of release, 2 weeks later displacing Baccara's 'Yes Sir, I Can Boogie' to take its rightful place at Number 1, where it stuck, immovable, throughout November 1977.

A father found

At least one member of Abba had her mind on something else at the end of that year. While the idea of appearing in the Australian movie was a new experience for Anni-Frid, who had ambitions to become an actress if and when Abba disbanded, she was diverted from giving the film much thought by a totally unexpected occurrence which instantly changed her world.

A story about Abba had appeared in a German magazine which mentioned Anni-Frid's unhappy early years and gave the name of her father, Alfred Haase, whom she had presumed to be dead. A German Abba fan had an uncle named Alfred Haase and, knowing that he had spent part of the war in Norway, asked whether he had ever met a Norwegian girl named Synni Lyngstad, Anni-Frid's mother who had died so tragically 30 years before.

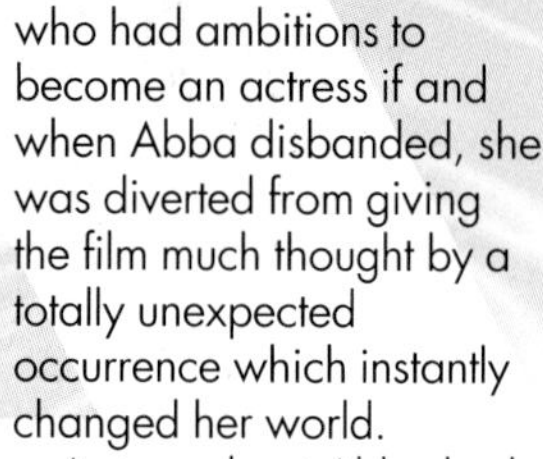

Anni-Frid (left) and Agnetha, a dynamic vocal duo.

Haase had tried to write to Synni, but the letters had never arrived. He had presumed that Synni was either dead or had no wish to become involved with him again, so he had settled down to life in Germany with the family he had had even before he was posted to Norway.

He had no idea at all that he had left Synni pregnant, and the discovery that he had a daughter in Sweden who was a world-famous pop star came as something of a shock. Surprise was replaced by delight, and before long a father and daughter who had not known of each other's existence were united.

Just before Christmas it was Agnetha's turn to be deliriously happy as she gave birth to her second child, Peter Christian Ulvaeus. That made it two perfect endings to another very successful year!

Yet another Number 1 single, 'The Name Of The Game'.

Chapter Five

A

CRACKS APPEAR

Although the final years of Björn, Benny, Agnetha and Anni-Frid's joint activity began with further spectacular successes, by the start of the Eighties the members of the group had undergone considerable changes in their personal lives.

Abba at one of the many press conferences held in 1978.

There was the distinct feeling that at least one quarter of Abba was wondering whether the immense success had been worth the heartbreak she was now experiencing.

But that was all some time away. The year of 1978 began with a bang—the new album, which was simply titled *The Album*, was instantly certified platinum, as the value of advance orders had topped £1 million ($1.5 million)! Abba's first release to enter the UK chart at Number 1, it dominated album sales in Britain for 7 weeks during a chart life which lasted for over a year.

This was a rather more weighty album than any of its predecessors. It was Abba's first new album since 1976 and everyone

B

was excited about the reception they knew it would get, especially as four of the songs were already known: 'The Name Of The Game' (the last UK Number 1) and the three songs from the mini-musical. Fans could be certain that part of it at least was highly desirable—but what about the tracks that no one had heard ? Their question was soon answered when the new single, 'Take A Chance On Me', was released, and became another UK Number 1, their seventh—and their last for over 2 years. This was track two on *The Album*.

The first track caused eyebrows to rise. 'Eagle' might not have sounded out of place on FM Rock Radio, and as such, was a brave move. Rather than being about the tribulations and triumphs of romance as so many of their other classics had been, 'Eagle' extolled the virtues of both the majestic bird of prey and the Californian country rock group the Eagles, whose latest album had been the immensely successful *Hotel California*. The video which accompanied 'Eagle' suggested that Abba's master songwriters might be changing direction.

The Album earned over £1 million ($1.5 million) in advance orders worldwide.

The Movie

Another reason for the vast advance orders for *The Album* was the release of the film to which it was

B

effectively the soundtrack album. Simply titled *The Movie*, it was doing incredible business in the UK, as it had already done in Australia, Sweden and Holland.

One reviewer described the film as "a 90-minute commercial for Abba", and critics overall were most unimpressed by its lack of a plot. Paying customers, however, were equally unimpressed by the views of critics, and packed cinemas to the point where the film was rated seventh among the box office hits of a year which included *Star Wars*, *Saturday Night Fever* and *Grease*.

Agnetha (left) and Anni-Frid with comedian Robert Hughes, who played the part of the disc jockey in *The Movie*.

Perhaps it didn't matter that the story line was so obviously bad—it's interesting to note that the executive producer of *The Movie*, Australian Reg Grundy, also gave us the TV soap *Neighbours*. Abba fans couldn't have cared less—they could be sure that there would be plenty of performances by their idols.

Conflicting paths

This was also to be the year when Abba made a serious effort to conquer the United States, virtually the only country of any note in the free world where they were not superstars. May 1978 was "Abba month", with a billboard on Sunset Strip (a privilege accorded to only the biggest—and richest—stars), a guest star spot on a

Abba flank Andy Gibb (in red) and Olivia Newton-John (third from right).

nationally networked TV special starring Olivia Newton-John and personal appearances on radio and television in as many places as possible. The idea was to transform both 'Take A Chance On Me' and *The Album* from moderate successes into smash hits.

While the results couldn't be called a total disaster

they weren't particularly good either, and it became clear that if Abba were to add America to the long list of countries where they were automatic chart-toppers, it would take much concerted effort over a long period and involve a lot of touring—which was a major bone of contention between Agnetha and the rest of the group. As a young mother with two small children, her maternal instincts made her feel guilty about seeing them infrequently and having to leave them too often to be looked after by others while she went to work. "It's such a lot of trouble to go on the road, and I've no intention of

> **"I'm as excited as anybody about going on tour, but for me, there's always a little sadness when I think about the children at home."**
> **Agnetha**

Frida (left) and Agnetha swing into action.

letting my children be brought up by somebody else. The family must come first," she said to the UK paper the *Sun* in 1978. "The first few months at school is when my daughter Linda needs me most. I'm as excited as anybody about going on tour, but for me, there's always a little sadness when I think about the children at home." This problem did not affect her colleagues in the same way—Anni-Frid didn't seem interested in having any more children, while Benny and Björn were keen to carry on with their attempt to conquer the charts of the whole world.

Cheek to cheek—togetherness for Mr and Mrs Andersson.

Seeds of discontent

It was apparently the second world tour which took place in 1979 that finally led to the group breaking up—although for the time being they continued to record with the same success as before.

Before they fell apart there were further notable triumphs, though their second and final single of 1978 was probably not one of them. 'Summer Night

B

City' was a rather ordinary song and performance by Abba's remarkable standards, and became the group's smallest hit for 3 years. Rather too disco-oriented for some tastes, it still reached the UK Top 5—hardly a failure, but disappointing none the less.

A month after its release, Benny and Frida finally got married after living together for 9 years. The wedding was kept a carefully guarded secret so that the couple wouldn't be besieged by the press and fans. At last, the fans thought, the group consisted of two happily married couples.

Still a couple—but it was to be curtains soon for Björn and Agnetha's marriage.

A

And I wanna know what's the name of the frame . . .

B

Breaking up is hard to do

They were in for a shock, however. Less than 3 months after Benny and Frida's wedding, Agnetha left Björn on Christmas Eve 1978. The group could have broken up right there, but when Stig Anderson pointed out forcibly that they were on the brink of becoming as big as the Beatles, they agreed to stay together for at least one more world tour, after which the situation would be reviewed again.

The formation of Abba was not a union between four totally compatible people, and had it not been for the fact that Benny and Björn were a songwriting team, it seems highly unlikely that Agnetha and Anni-Frid would ever have worked together—the sophisticated Frida was a complete contrast to the more straightforward and direct Agnetha, and no doubt the differences between their characters were simply reflections of their greatly differing back-grounds.

As Björn said: "We're human, we argue like most normal people, and that goes for the women, too. But if our off-days had taken on the proportions the press has suggested, we simply couldn't work together any longer."

Carrying on

The year of 1979 began with another big hit single, 'Chiquitita', which was expected to add to Abba's long list of chart-topping singles but ultimately couldn't quite outsell Blondie's 'Heart Of Glass', and peaked at Number 2 in the UK. None the less it was a definite improvement on 'Summer Night City'—and soon afterwards a world tour which would include selected dates in North America was announced.

Before the tour began, Abba recorded a TV special in Switzerland as part of BBC TV's *Snowtime Special* series which also featured Boney M and included guest appearances by Kate Bush and Roxy Music, after which Frida began to further her ambitions as an actress by appearing in a Swedish movie, *Walk On Water*. At the time she said, "Although it's a small part, I

'Angeleyes' led to confusion with Roxy Music's 'Angel Eyes', and didn't reach Number 1.

feel it could lead to better things, but I've no intention of abandoning my singing career." Meanwhile, Björn and Benny were putting the finishing touches to the new album, *Voulez Vous*, which the group would be promoting on the tour.

A week before the *Voulez Vous* album reached the record shops, one of its tracks, 'Does Your Mother Know' was released as a single. This caused some controversy among the fans as, for the first time on the A side of an Abba single, Björn was lead vocalist rather than one or both of the girls. Still, it was a Top 5 hit in the UK and certainly drew attention to the album, which entered the UK chart at Number 1 when it was released in May 1979, staying at the top for a month. The album also included Abba's next single, which coupled the title track and 'Angeleyes' and reached Number 3. Many fans felt it could have been another Number 1 had it not been for the fact that initially 'Angeleyes' was treated as the A side. At almost exactly the same time, Roxy Music recorded and released a single of a totally different song also titled 'Angel Eyes' and the confusion this caused almost certainly prevented both songs going higher in the chart. Eventually both sides of the Abba single were treated equally and it was promoted as a double A side, but by then it was too late to scale the ultimate chart heights.

New markets, new hits

While last-minute preparations for the tour were being finalized, several major new markets opened up for the group—in South America. An employee of the label which released their records in Argentina had written new Spanish

Reaching for the sky on the 1979 world tour, which turned out to be Abba's final international trek.

lyrics to 'Chiquitita', and the group recorded these new words over the original instrumental backing. This version of 'Chiquitita' became a smash hit in much of the South American continent.

In September 1979 Abba started the tour which would prove to be their last with their first-ever live dates in North America. This was inevitably going to be only a token visit; with so many major cities in the United States and Canada it would take many months, even years, to cover them all. Nevertheless, almost 150,000 people saw Abba, and the general feeling was that this first toe dipped into the huge lake that is America was a reasonable success.

Next came the European leg of the tour, which took in shows in eight countries including Scandinavia, Germany and France, followed by a ten-date British section which included six nights at London's Wembley Arena, where the nearly 50,000 seats available had been sold in a matter of hours several months earlier.

By this time, Agnetha (left) and Björn (right) were always separated in photographs.

Before the British dates began, there was the inevitable new single, 'Gimme! Gimme! Gimme! (A Man After Midnight)', which was released to promote yet another new album, *Greatest Hits Volume 2*. The Abba hit machine was working at full power, and although 'Gimme! Gimme! Gimme!' once again failed to make the Number 1 spot, peaking when it reached the Top 3, the album made up for any disappointments by becoming Abba's fifth in succession to reach the UK Number 1 spot—although, unlike *The Album* and *Voulez Vous*, it didn't enter the chart at the top, being delayed for a week by Fleetwood Mac's long-awaited double album, *Tusk*.

Still alive

Predictably, the British shows were a huge success, combining the expected barrage of classic hits with some less predictable items which included Agnetha

B

accompanying herself on piano to sing 'I'm Still Alive' (a song many felt came from the heart in view of her separation from Björn) and Frida singing a song from the *Voulez Vous* album, 'I Have A Dream', accompanied by a choir of small children.

Abba had gone to some pains to ensure that these shows were memorable, using a futuristic stage set with a moving pyramid backdrop in their long set and wearing eye-catching spandex costumes (which suited Agnetha and Frida better than Benny or Björn!).

Frida and Agnetha worship Abba's very own guitar hero, Lasse Wellander.

Overleaf: The foursome on stage during the world tour.

moog
moog

Benny demonstrates the dimensions of a catch on a Caribbean fishing trip.

After such a successful year, which had included two huge-selling Number 1 albums and four Top 5 hit singles, some fans might have expected Abba to rest on their laurels before the final part of the tour in early 1980, which would take in Japan—another country where the group were immensely popular. But more chart activity was ahead for Abba before the new decade got under way, with the release as a single of 'I Have A Dream', which had been such a success in the live performances with the children's choirs, together with a version of 'Chiquitita' which had been recorded live at Wembley. This became the group's fifth single to reach the Top 5 in Britain in 1979, an incredible achievement—though 'I Have A Dream', like 'Chiquitita', lost its momentum when it reached Number 2.

Gracias por la musica

With most of the tour over, the male half of Abba went on a working holiday to the Caribbean to write songs for the next album while Agnetha and Anni-Frid remained in Sweden, recording Spanish lyrics to a complete album of Abba songs in order to satisfy the growing demand for the group's music in South America. The result of this was an album titled *Gracias Por La Musica* (which, confusingly, translates as "thank you for the music" although the tracks on it are not the ones on the album of the same name released in the rest of the world in 1983). An immense seller in the Hispanic-speaking world, *Gracias Por La Musica* was even released in Britain

The album with specially written lyrics in Spanish. Designed for the South American market, it was a massive hit.

"It was quite true that our lives were reflected in the lyrics—though it doesn't mean 'The Winner Takes It All' is autobiographical; neither Agnetha nor I were winners in our divorce." Björn

although, perhaps not surprisingly, it failed to break into the album chart.

It wasn't until mid-1980 that a new Abba single was released. 'The Winner Takes It All', a thoughtful ballad with lead vocal by Agnetha, restored the group to the top of the UK singles chart, becoming their eighth Number 1 and their

A

eighteenth hit single. The song seemed to reflect the changes that had taken place in the relationships within the group, but some years later Björn confessed a journalist: "It was quite true that our lives were reflected in the lyrics—one can't help that—though it doesn't mean a song like 'The Winner Takes It All' is autobiographical; neither Agnetha nor I were winners in our divorce."

Super troupers

The track was included on the next album, released at the end of a year in which the four had adopted a relatively low profile. As usual, the album's title track was released as a single as a taster for the main event, and 'Super Trouper' quickly

B

Abba with circus performers on the set for the video of 'Super Trouper'. Inspired by and named after the huge theatrical lights, it evoked the sound of a fairground.

A

B

became Abba's ninth (and last)UK Number 1 single. It would probably have stayed at the top for longer than 3 weeks had not John Lennon's '(Just Like) Starting Over' replaced it in the wave of public sympathy that followed his murder. Abba's song was inspired by the giant spotlights used on stage by rock stars, and the memorable video featured circus performers, in keeping with the tune's fairground rhythm.

The *Super Trouper* album entered the UK chart at Number 1, the third time Abba had achieved this feat. Widely regarded as one of the group's finest albums (maybe the very best), it captured them at the height of their powers. A brilliant selection of songs included the two most recent Number 1 hits, two aimed at the dance market ('Lay All Your Love On Me' and 'On And On And On'), a couple of clever slabs of nostalgia ('The Way Old Friends Do' and 'Happy New Year'), and a piece of perfect soft rock which could have come from the heady hippy days of the Sixties, 'Our Last Summer'.

Björn singing 'Does Your Mother Know' on tour—the only time neither girl sang lead vocals.

If this was to be Abba's farewell to the world of popular music they could hardly have chosen a better way of saying goodbye. However, there was still quite a lot more music to come from the group as they gradually disintegrated over the next 2 years.

Chapter Six

A

THE END OF ABBA?

The break-up of Agnetha and Björn's marriage had fatally damaged the group and at the beginning of 1981 two more nails were driven into Abba's coffin.

In January Björn got married again—having embarked upon his relationship with new wife, Lena Kallersjö, only days after Agnetha's unhappy departure—and in February Benny and Anni-Frid announced that they would be getting a divorce. Only 2½ years after Benny had married Anni-Frid he had fallen for a TV presenter, Mona Norklit.

B

The cracks widen

The effect on the group was not instant, and they appeared together on the highly rated *Dick Cavett Show* on US TV, on which they played several songs live. However, it was becoming clear that their dreams of making it big in the States would probably have to be forgotten, as the personal lives of each of the group members were of far greater concern to them than their joint careers as international pop stars. As Benny remarked, "I've no idea how long we can continue. I wouldn't dare to make a guess. It's a matter of will and potential, wanting to do something, but I really enjoy what I do—without work, life would be meaningless. It's the major part of my life." Björn also felt uncertain: "I don't know how much longer we can go on, but we don't make any long-range plans any more."

> **"I've no idea how long we can continue. I wouldn't dare to make a guess. It's a matter of will and potential, wanting to do something, but I really enjoy what I do—without work, life would be meaningless."**
>
> **Benny**

The stream of new products from the prolific pens of Benny and Björn had also slowed to a trickle, and in the second half of the year 'Lay All Your Love On Me', another track from the *Super Trouper* album, was released in the UK as the new Abba single. It had already achieved considerable success in the US, where it had topped the dance chart, and as a result

'Lay All Your Love On Me', the biggest selling 12-inch single ever when it was released.

was pushed out in Britain in 12-inch format. Whatever market it was aimed at, British record buyers immediately dashed out to buy it, although it would perhaps have achieved a higher chart placing had it also been available as a regular 7-inch single. Even so, its Top 10 position made it at the time the most successful 12-inch single in UK chart history, while another *Super Trouper* track, 'On And On And On', also enjoyed success in the US dance chart. But personal tensions were overshadowing chart success, for in October, Benny and Mona

Abba on stage at the beginning of the Eighties. Despite growing internal tensions, the four still performed together regularly.

formalized their relationship by getting married.

Stars on 45

This was also the year of the Stars On 45 explosion. A Dutch musician turned record producer conceived the idea of recording a medley of cover versions of hits originally recorded by the Beatles which sounded very similar to the real thing, apart from the fact that they were linked by a metronomic disco rhythm. It was an obvious move to adopt a similar approach with a medley of eight Abba songs, and the result was a UK Top 20 hit.

While it was gratifying that their hits should be used to such effect, Björn and Benny had far more exciting news—they had been invited to a meeting with Tim Rice, Britain's most successful lyricist, whose collaborations with Andrew Lloyd Webber had produced a string of international hit musicals such as *Joseph And His Amazing Technicolour Dreamcoat*, *Jesus Christ Superstar* and *Evita*. Rice was interested in pursuing a new idea for a stage musical, and wanted to know whether Benny and Björn would be interested in writing tunes to his lyrics. Of course they were!

The end of the year brought a brand new single, 'One Of Us', the first track to be released from what would turn out to be Abba's final original album. Released also as the group's first picture disc

Abba's last UK Top 3 hit, 'One Of Us', which heralded the end of the group's domination of the UK singles charts.

single, it was a substantial hit, reaching the UK Top 3, while the new album, *The Visitors*, reached the shops a week later. Even if their singles were no longer guaranteed to top the charts, Abba's albums undoubtedly were, and *The Visitors* became yet another album to enter the charts at Number 1.

The songs on the album indicated that Björn and Benny were adopting a different and perhaps more mature approach to their songwriting activities—'When All Is Said And Done' seemed to suggest resignation at the end of a romance (or could it have been written because it was clear that Abba's days were numbered?), and 'Two For The Price Of One' was regarded as most peculiar, apparently telling the story of a lonely hearts advertisement offering not only a girlfriend, but also her mother! But the group were pleased with the album; as Frida remarked, "Since our divorces, we have become more mature, and our style is progressing more quickly than before.

"Since our divorces, our style is progressing more quickly than before. *The Visitors* reflects this evolution and maturity."
Frida

The Visitors reflects this evolution and maturity."

New ventures

Within the first 10 days of 1982 there were two additions to the extended Abba family as Emma, the first child to result from Björn and Lena's marriage, was born, to be swiftly followed by Ludwig, son of Benny and Mona. At the start of February, a second

single, 'Head Over Heels', was released from the new album. This was the group's least successful single since 1975, failing to reach the UK Top 20 at all. It was not that it was below Abba's usual standard—it just seemed that in the minds of many record buyers the group had simply passed their sell-by date.

Frida, meanwhile, had been working on a solo album, her first in the English language, although she had released three in Swedish during the Seventies. The album, *Something's Going On*, was produced by Phil Collins, who was at the time emerging as a solo star after many years of success with Genesis. Frida had been particularly struck by *Face Value*, a solo album by Collins which had topped the UK chart and was composed of songs generated by the break-up of his marriage.

Frida's album wasn't a flop, but its chart life was extremely brief compared with the performance she had come to expect from Abba albums—a mere 7 weeks and a highest position just inside the UK Top 20. With songs written by several well-known stars, including Bryan Ferry, Giorgio Moroder, Stephen Bishop and Collins himself, *Something's Going On* was

'Head Over Heels' was Abba's least successful single in 7 years.

Frida's first English language solo album, *Something's Going On*, was released in 1982.

a good début solo album, but it lacked the magic and chemistry which made Abba records so exceptional.

Finally a flop

Meanwhile, Björn and Benny had written two new songs, 'Just Like That' and 'I Am The City', which had been recorded as possible future Abba tracks and were perhaps intended for inclusion on a forthcoming double compilation album which would include all the group's past hits, plus, of course, a couple of new songs which would be released as singles.

In fact, neither of those two new songs appeared on *The Singles—The First Ten Years*, the double album released on November 5, 1982, although there were indeed two songs which had not been heard before. The single of 'The Day Before You Came' was released as the usual preview of a new album, but this one was not much of a hit, failing even to reach the UK Top 30. (When British electropop duo Blancmange released their cover version of the song in 1984 it was a bigger hit than Abba's original had been.)

The song's failure as the new Abba single made no difference whatsoever to the success of the album, which included 23 Abba singles from 'Ring Ring' to 'Under Attack', the other new song on the collection.

'The Day Before You Came', a bigger hit for Blancmange (who covered the song in 1984) than for Abba 2 years before.

Ascending out of the spotlight—for ever?

By its second week in the UK racks the album was at Number 1, although it was prevented from reigning supreme for any longer by John Lennon again—the late Beatle was becoming rather a nuisance to Abba, this time holding them off the top slot over the Christmas holiday with *The John Lennon Collection*, a compilation of hits. The Christmas period was a time when the Abba record

Stig Anderson (left) joins Abba as they receive more precious metal in the form of platinum.

had been expected to sell prodigiously.

This was Abba's last album when they were still active as a group, and like all the others it went directly to the top of the charts around the world—but not

in the US. However, as Björn said, "Most people would say we've conquered the USA

"Most people would say we've conquered the USA because our albums have gone platinum." **Björn**

because our albums have gone platinum. If you consider the States conquered, then there's nowhere they don't play Abba, except maybe China, but I don't think they have many record players there. If they had, they'd be playing Abba."

At the start of December, 'Under Attack' was released as a single, and performed slightly more impressively than 'The Day Before You Came' by reaching the UK Top 30—but after that there was deafening silence on the Abba front until the middle of the year.

Agnetha goes solo

In June 1983 Agnetha's first solo album with English lyrics was released. Like Anni-Frid, Agnetha had made solo albums before but all had been in Swedish, and so were of limited interest outside Scandinavia.

Wrap Your Arms Around Me was produced by Mike Chapman, who had enjoyed considerable success working in partnership with Nicky Chinn, creating hits for a variety of famous acts during the early Seventies including the Sweet, Mud, Smokie, Suzi Quatro and others. After moving to the States in the late Seventies, Chapman continued to produce hits on his own, especially the many international successes achieved by Blondie.

Unfortunately, Chapman was not able to produce any similar chart-toppers for Agnetha, although her album, like Anni-Frid's, briefly reached the UK Top 20. Even so it was quite a busy year for Agnetha, who also performed the theme song of a Swedish feature film, *P & B*, and made an appearance in another Swedish movie, *Raskenstam*.

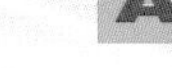

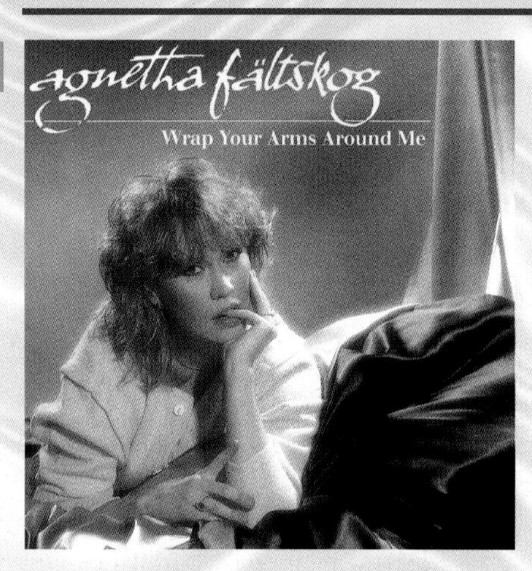

Who could resist such an invitation from such a woman?

Most of 1984 was even quieter, with just about the only item of note being Frida's second solo album, *Shine*, which was produced by the famed Steve Lillywhite, who had been responsible for numerous hit albums by such artists as U2, Simple Minds and Peter Gabriel.

Despite the fact that it included a track written for her by Benny and Björn titled 'Slowly', the album was considerably less successful than *Something's Going On* and seems to have effectively ended Frida's ambitions towards becoming an international solo star. Nevertheless, she has continued to make records for the local Scandinavian market with some success.

The stamp of success
Later that year, the Swedish post office paid Abba a very rare compliment—they issued a set of commemorative stamps featuring illustrious Swedish musicians, and the sole representatives of pop music in the series were, of course, Abba.

Following the success of *The Singles* at Christmas 1982, it was inevitable that another Abba album would be released for Christmas 1983. *Thank You For The Music* made a minor dent in the UK album chart, even though it included absolutely nothing new.

B

Chess

The big Abba news of 1984 came right at the end of the year with the unveiling of the *Chess* album, which had taken up much of Benny and Björn's time over the previous 2 years. This was the musical on which they had been working with Tim Rice, and its title provides a clue as to just how unlikely a subject had been chosen for a musical. The theme concerned the game of chess, centring on a championship contest between an American and a Russian. It had clearly been inspired by the real-life world chess championship between American Bobby Fischer and his Russian opponent, Boris Spassky, which took place in Iceland in 1972. This was several years before the breakdown of communism in Eastern Europe, and the Fischer v. Spassky contest was regarded as a reflection of the Cold War which had divided the world over the previous 25 years.

The plot of the musical concerned a fictitious Russian chess champion

Björn (right) with Murray Head, one of the stars of the *Chess* album.

who fell in love with a woman from the free world, and the political implications which resulted from such a relationship.

The musical included two major hit songs. The first, 'One Night In Bangkok', sung by Murray Head, reached the Top 10 in Britain, was a big hit in many other countries, especially in Europe, and also reached the Top 3 in America, a considerable achievement. The second, 'I Know Him So Well', a duet between Elaine Paige and Barbara Dickson, was a massive hit in Britain, where it topped the singles chart for a month at the start of 1985, and went on to become one of the most frequently played tracks on British pop radio. The *Chess* soundtrack double album was also a fair success (although maybe not by Abba standards)—it reached the UK Top 10 and the US Top 50. *Chess* went on stage in London in 1986 at the Prince Edward Theatre, where it ran for some years to considerable acclaim.

Another solo album

In 1985 Agnetha's second solo album, *Eyes Of A Woman*, was produced, like Anni-Frid's *Something's Going On*, by a performer rather than a studio wizard. Eric Stewart was one of the founders and remains one of the leaders of 10cc, the

A rare picture of Benny (left) playing guitar with his Abba colleagues.

B

highly successful rock group from Manchester. Apart from producing the album, he contributed several songs he had written (as well as co-writing 'I Won't Let You Go' with Agnetha). Other writers included Jeff Lynne (founder of Electric Light Orchestra and latterly one of the Travelin' Wilburys), Geoff Downes (once of Buggles and later of Yes) and Justin Hayward (hit songwriter of the Moody Blues).

Opus 10?

During a promotional interview for *Eyes Of A Woman*—which was less successful than *Wrap Your Arms Around Me* but more successful than Frida's *Shine*—Agnetha remarked that while she had no regrets about Abba's remarkable past career she certainly didn't want to restart it, although she didn't rule out the possibility of another Abba album at some point in the future. At the end of the year, there was indeed more talk of a new Abba album, which would be their tenth (not including compilations) and thus had a working title of *Opus 10*. It hasn't happened yet. . . .

Winding down

There was hardly any Abba activity during 1986, although 1987 at least featured a third solo album from Agnetha,

Agnetha embarked on a solo career—but it was far less successful than Abba's world domination.

B

Abba the way their millions of fans remember them—a great stage show with wonderful music.

I Stand Alone. Once again, a performer was chosen as producer, Peter Cetera of the group Chicago. While the album reached the UK chart for just 1 week, it must have convinced Agnetha that becoming a successful international solo artist was tough, because since then she too has confined herself to recording almost totally for the Scandinavian market.

The only item of note for Abba fans in 1988 was a new compilation album of their work, *The Collection Volume 2*. This included a number of live tracks never previously released, which

were part of a projected live Abba album mentioned a couple of years before, but never released. The double album also included another complete Abba album which had never previously been released outside Sweden, the group's very first LP from 1973, *Ring Ring*.

Sadly, few realized that so much new and unheard material by their favourite group was available, and the double album seems never to have even approached the UK chart.

Under the Polygram umbrella

The second half of the 1980s was a period when everyone seemed to have forgotten about Abba, and things might never have changed had not Stig Anderson, who by then was approaching retirement age, decided to sell Polar Music (whose main asset was the hit-packed Abba catalogue) to Polygram, one of the six major corporations which dominate the world record industry.

During their hit-making years, Abba had been signed to many different labels around the world, rather than owing their allegiance to one company worldwide. This approach seemed at the time to have more advantages than drawbacks, as Polar Music would doubtless earn more in the way of advance

Björn in the foreground for a change.

A

payments and the various competing companies (Atlantic, part of WEA, in America; Epic, allied to CBS, in Britain; and other rivals in other parts of the world) would all try to make Abba's releases as big as possible in the hope that when it was time to renew the deal with Stig, he might allow them to release Abba records in more of the world than they already controlled.

This was probably the way things were in the first 10 years of the group's international emergence, but by the end of the Eighties, when accountants and lawyers who knew little about hit potential were largely running the record business, companies were unwilling to invest in an act whose work they did not control all over the world. So when Polygram offered Stig a large amount of money in return for Polar Music (and therefore Abba's catalogue) world-wide, in his position he didn't feel he had much alternative but to accept.

Abba disintegrates

The change of ownership began on the first day of 1990, although it wasn't

The two married couples swap places in the line-up after they become two divorced couples.

B

until 2 years later, when the last of the existing licensing deals had come to an end, that much could be done about reviving interest in one of the biggest and most successful groups in the entire history of modern popular music. The other major event of the year came just before Christmas, when Agnetha married her second husband, a surgeon named Tomas Sonnenfeld. (The marriage didn't last long, however; the two were divorced in 1993.)

The first years of the Nineties saw the continued gradual disintegration of the group as they drifted apart. The early highlight of 1992 occurred when Anni-Frid joined Roxette on stage in Zurich for an encore of 'Money Money Money'.

Roxette, a duo of vocalist Marie Fredriksson and songwriter Per Gessle, also came from Sweden, and must have been inspired by Abba's example in their aim to dominate the world's charts—an ambition which, it must be said, they came close to achieving with four singles which reached the US Top 3 in under 18 months: both 'The Look' and 'Listen to Your Heart' were Number 1 hits in 1989, while 'Dangerous' and a third Number 1, 'It Must Have Been Love', continued their chart-storming progress in 1990.

The albums reissued

During the spring of 1992 all Abba's original albums were reissued by Polygram, and for the first time, both the *Ring Ring* album and *Abba Live* were complete and freely available. The live album was particularly interesting, containing concert performances from both the 1977 and 1979 tours, along with four songs performed on the 1981 American TV show hosted by Dick Cavett.

By June 1992 Erasure were at the top of the UK charts with the *Abba-esque* EP, Björn Again were filling concert halls all over the world, and Polygram were preparing to release *Abba Gold*. When this "greatest hits" album topped the charts around the world, it was obvious that Abba, far from being forgotten, were again one of the most popular groups in the world.

CHRONOLOGY

A

1970

Spring	Benny and Björn become a songwriting team.
Autumn	The four future members of Abba first play together in public.

1971

July	Björn and Agnetha get married.

1972

Autumn	The four future members of Abba release their first single.

1973

February	'Ring Ring' is rejected by the Swedish Eurovision jury.

1974

April	'Waterloo' wins Eurovision and becomes Abba's first UK Number 1.

1976

January	'Mamma Mia' becomes their second Number 1.
May	'Fernando' is their third UK Number 1 single and *Greatest Hits* their first UK Number 1 album.
June	Abba perform 'Dancing Queen' at the marriage of the King of Sweden.
September	'Dancing Queen' becomes their fourth UK Number 1 single.

1977

January	*Arrival* becomes their second UK Number 1 album.
April	'Knowing Me, Knowing You' is Abba's fifth UK Number 1 single.
November	'The Name Of The Game' is their sixth UK Number 1 single, as Abba play their first world tour.
Winter	Frida meets the father whom she thought was dead.

1978

February	*The Album* becomes Abba's second consecutive UK Number 1 LP, while 'Take A Chance On Me' is their seventh UK Number 1 single, and *Abba—The Movie* is released.
October	Benny and Anni-Frid finally get married.
December	Agnetha and Björn separate.

1979

May — Abba's *Voulez-Vous* becomes their fourth UK Number 1 album.

November — Abba play their second and last world tour, as *Greatest Hits Vol 2* inevitably tops the world's album charts.

1980

August — 'The Winner Takes It All' becomes Abba's eighth UK Number 1 single.

November — 'Super Trouper' not only becomes the group's ninth UK Number 1 single, but is also the title track of their sixth UK Number 1 album.

1981

December — *The Visitors* is Abba's seventh UK Number 1 album.

1982

November — Abba's eighth UK Number 1 album is *The Singles—The First Ten Years*, after which they effectively break up.

1982–4 — Agnetha and Anni-Frid attempt barely successful solo careers, while Benny and Björn write the musical *Chess* with Tim Rice.

1985

February — 'I Know Him So Well', a song from *Chess* sung by Elaine Paige and Barbara Dickson, becomes the tenth UK Number 1 single written by Benny and Björn.

1992

June — Erasure top the singles chart with their 'Abba-esque' EP.

September — *Abba Gold* restores the group to the top of the world's charts, selling 4.5 million copies worldwide even before the album's release in the US.

DISCOGRAPHY

ALBUMS

Ring Ring
1973
UK: Polydor 843 642-2
Chart: UK–, US –

Waterloo
1974
UK: Polydor 843 643-2
Chart: UK 28, US 145

Abba
1975
UK: Polydor 831 596-2
Chart: UK 13, US 174

Greatest Hits
1975
UK: Epic CDEPC 10017
Chart: UK 1, US 48

Arrival
1976
UK: Polydor 821 319-2
Chart: UK1, US 20

The Album
1977
UK: Polydor 821 217-2
Chart: UK1 US 14

Voulez-Vous
1979
UK: Polydor 821 320-2
Chart: UK1, US 19

Greatest Hits Vol 2
1979
UK: Polydor
800 012-2
Chart: UK 1, US 46

Gracias Por La Musica
1980
Japan: Polydor
POCP 2209
Chart: UK –, US –

Super Trouper
1980
UK: Polydor 800 023-2
Chart: UK 1, US 17

The Visitors
1981
UK: Polydor 800 011-2
Chart: UK 1, US 29

The Singles—The First Ten Years
1982
UK: Polydor 810 050-2
US: Polygrqm 810050-2
Chart: UK 1, US 62

Abba Live
1986
UK: Polydor 829 951-2
Chart: UK –, US –

Abba Gold
1992
UK: Polydor 517 007-2
Chart: UK 1 (Not released in US)

More Abba Gold
1993
UK: Polydor 519 353-2
Chart: UK 16 (still in chart at time of writing)

SINGLES

'Ring Ring'
1973
Chart UK 32, US –

'Waterloo'
1974
Chart: UK 1, US 6

'Honey Honey'
1974
Chart: UK –, US 27

'So Long'
1974
Chart: UK –, US –

'I Do, I Do, I Do, I Do, I Do'
1975
Chart: UK 38, US 15

'S.O.S.'
1975
Chart: UK 6, US 15

'Mamma Mia'
1975
Chart: UK 1, US 32

'Fernando'
1976
Chart: UK 1, US 13

'Dancing Queen'
1976
Chart: UK 1, US 1

'Money, Money, Money' *1976*
Chart: UK 3, US 56

'Knowing Me, Knowing You'
1977
Chart: UK 1, US 14

'The Name Of The Game'
1977
Chart: UK 1, US 12

'Take A Chance On Me' *1977*
Chart: UK 1, US 3

'Summer Night City'
1978
Chart: UK 5, US –

'Chiquitita'
1979
Chart: UK 2, US 29

'Does Your Mother Know'
1979
Chart: UK 4, US 19

'Voulez-Vous'/ 'Angeleyes'
1979
Chart: UK 3, US 64

'Gimme! Gimme! Gimme! (A Man After Midnight)'
1979
Chart: UK 3, US –

'I Have A Dream'
1979
Chart: UK 2, US –

'The Winner Takes It All'
1980
Chart: UK 1, US 8

'Super Trouper'
1980
Chart: UK 1, US 45

'Lay All Your Love On Me'/'On And On And On' (12-inch)
1981
Chart: UK 7, US 90

'One Of Us'
1981
Chart: UK 3, US –

'Head Over Heels'/ 'The Visitors'
1982
Chart: UK 25, US 63

'The Day Before You Came'
1982
Chart: UK 32, US –

'Under Attack'
1982
Chart: UK 26, US –

'Thank You for The Music'
1983
Chart: UK 33, US –

VIDEOGRAPHY

Abba Gold
1992
Polygram Video

More Abba Gold
1993
Polygram Video

INDEX

All page numbers in *italics* refer to illustrations

Acknowledgements

All photographs, including the cover photograph, supplied by London Features International, except for page 44, © BBC. Every effort has been made to trace and clear copyright of the images reproduced in this book. If any omissions have occurred an acknowledgement will be made in future editions.

B